Pony Club

Pony Club

Sandy Creek
NEW YORK

Sandy Creek
NEW YORK

An Imprint of Sterling Publishing
387 Park Avenue South
New York, NY 10016

Editor: Amanda Askew
Designer: Izzy Langridge

Picture credits
(t=top, b=bottom, l=left, r=right, c=center, fc=front cover)

All images are courtesy of Bob Langrish images unless stated below.
Alamy 36 Kenneth Ginn, 44br Norman Freelan, 60tr David L. Moore – Oahu, 60br ableimages, 64br Kumar Sriskandan, 73tr PCJones, 73bl The Photolibrary Wales

DK Images 10bl, 10br Kit Houghton, 13t Dorling Kindersley, 13bl David Handley, 14 Kit Houghton, 17t Dorling Kindersley, 37br Bob Langrish, 38 (water brush) Peter Chadwick, (metal curry comb) Andy Crawford and Kit Houghton, 39l (1,2,3,4,5) Kit Houghton, 19br Kit Houghton, 21 (1) Dorling Kindersley (2) Andy Crawford and Kit Houghton, (3) Andy Crawford and Kit Houghton, (4) Andy Crawford and Kit Houghton, (6) Andy Crawford and Kit Houghton, 45br David Handley, br Kit Houghton, 8 Dorling Kindersley, 10r Andy Crawford, 71l Kit Houghton, 72br Dorling Kindersley, 63tr Bob Langrish, 68r John Henderson, 69br Andy Crawford, 70r Bob Langrish, 71br Andy Crawford, 79b Dorling Kindersley
Dreamstime 1 Asso59, 38 (Rubber Curry Comb) Ad Van Brunschot, (body brush) Stanko07
Getty 30 Melissa Farlow
Shutterstock 1b Peter Baxter, 16 Tamara Didenko, 17t Tihis, 26 Groomee, 31b Pavel Kosek, 31t Lilac Mountain, 32t Maksym Protsenko, 32bl Chrislofoto, 33 (ragwort) Peter Wollinga, (yew) Joe Gough, (bracken) Dariush M, (foxglove) J and S Photography, (rhododendron) Brykaylo Yuriy, (deadly nightshade) Sue Robinson, (horsetail) LianeM, 33bc Judy Kennamer, 34tr alessandro0770, 36tr marekuliasz, 38 (hoofpick) Cathleen A Clapper, (dandy brush) Ad van Brunschot, (sponge) Cretolamna, 41 (5) Mirecea BEZERGHEANU, 43cr Dennis Donohue, 47tr (injection) Kondrashov Mlkhail Evgenevich, (sky) Serg64, 65tl cynoclub

ISBN 978-1-4351-4412-5

For information about custom editions, special sales, and premium and corporate purchases, please contact Sterling Special Sales at 800-805-5489 or specialsales@sterlingpublishing.com.

Manufactured in Guandong, China
Lot #:
2 4 6 8 10 9 7 5 3 1
09/12

Words in **bold** are explained in the glossary on page 110.

Remember! Children must always wear appropriate clothing, including a riding hat, and follow safety guidelines when handling or riding horses and ponies.

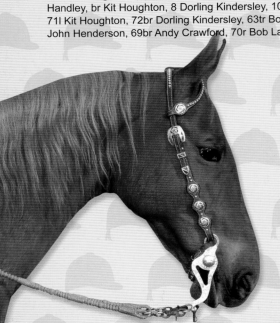

Contents

Learn to Ride

Learn to Ride

Mounting and dismounting

Mounting means getting on a pony and dismounting means getting off it. To help you get on the pony, you can use a mounting block or someone can give you a **leg up**—but you also need to be able to do it without help.

Using a Mounting Block

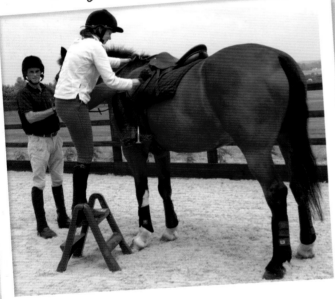

Standing on a block helps when the pony is tall or if you can't jump high. It also prevents you from pulling the saddle over as you spring up.

Getting a Leg Up

To get a leg up, first ask someone to hold the lower part of your left leg. Then when you're ready, they can push you up as you spring off your right foot.

Dismounting

To dismount safely, take both feet out of the stirrups. Lean forward to the pony's left side, and swing your right leg over the saddle and the pony's back. Take care not to catch it with your toe, and slide to the ground, landing on both feet.

Mounting Without Help

1. Stand on the pony's left side, facing its tail. Hold the **reins** in your left hand.
2. Put your left foot in the **stirrup iron**.
3. Spring up off your right foot, catch hold of the saddle with your right hand and swing your right leg over the saddle.
4. Sit down gently.
5. Turn the front of the right stirrup iron outwards and put your right foot in.

In the Saddle

When you first sit on a pony, it may feel strange. Try to relax and sit comfortably. Keep your back straight and let your legs hang down naturally. Your stirrups will be about the right length if the bottom of the iron is level with your instep.

Top Tip!
Before you set off, get someone to check the **girth** is tight enough.

Adjusting the Stirrups

You can adjust the length of the stirrups by pulling up the end of the leather and sliding the buckle up or down. Make sure the prong is in the hole. Pull down the underside of the leather so the buckle is under the buckle guard.

At first, you may need help finding the stirrup with your right foot.

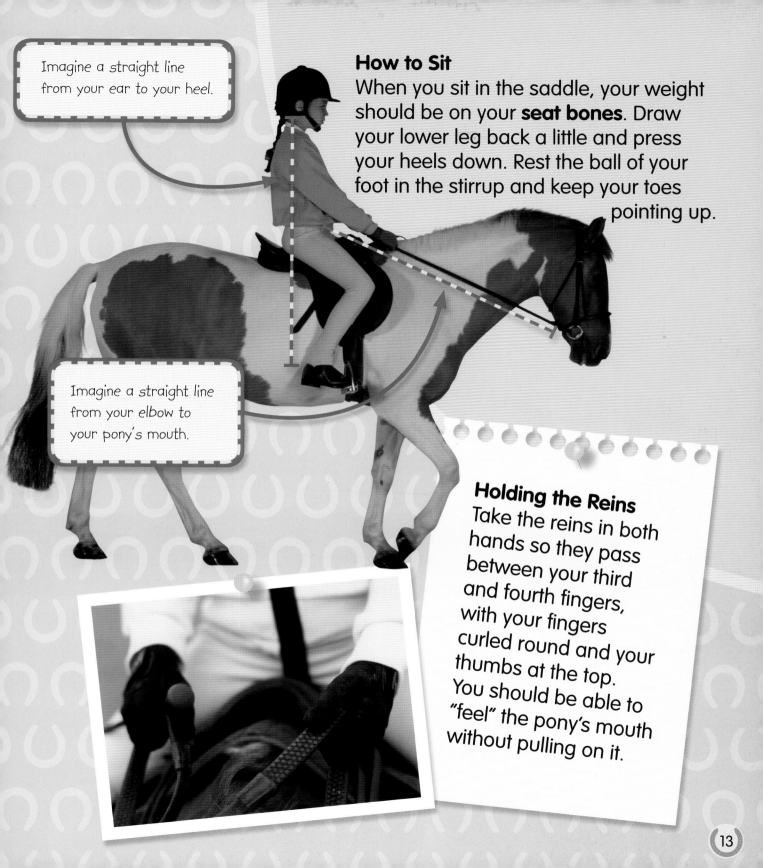

Imagine a straight line from your ear to your heel.

Imagine a straight line from your elbow to your pony's mouth.

How to Sit

When you sit in the saddle, your weight should be on your **seat bones**. Draw your lower leg back a little and press your heels down. Rest the ball of your foot in the stirrup and keep your toes pointing up.

Holding the Reins

Take the reins in both hands so they pass between your third and fourth fingers, with your fingers curled round and your thumbs at the top. You should be able to "feel" the pony's mouth without pulling on it.

Riding at Walk

To tell a horse or pony what to do, you use signals called "**aids**." You give these signals with your legs, hands, seat, body weight, and voice. These are called "natural aids." Experienced riders can also give signals with whips and spurs, and these are called "artificial aids."

Keep contact with the pony's mouth with the reins, but don't hold your arms and hands stiffly.

Walking Forward

To tell a pony to walk forward, shorten your reins slightly and press your lower legs into its sides. You can also say "Walk on" in an encouraging tone of voice. As soon as the pony moves forward, ease the pressure with your legs, but keep them touching the pony's sides. Let your hands follow the movement of the pony's head.

Tapping a pony on the **quarters** with a long schooling whip will tell it to move its hindquarters over.

Spurs are fitted over riding boots. When they are used correctly, they can make a horse or pony carry out actions with only the slightest pressure.

How to Halt

To stop, press your legs into the pony's sides, but hold the reins firmly so it cannot move forward. You can also say "Whoa." When the pony has halted, release the pressure from your legs and hands, and give it a pat on the neck and say "Good pony."

Learning to Trot

Trotting can be tricky, but it will become much easier with plenty of practice. Soon, you will be able to do it without thinking!

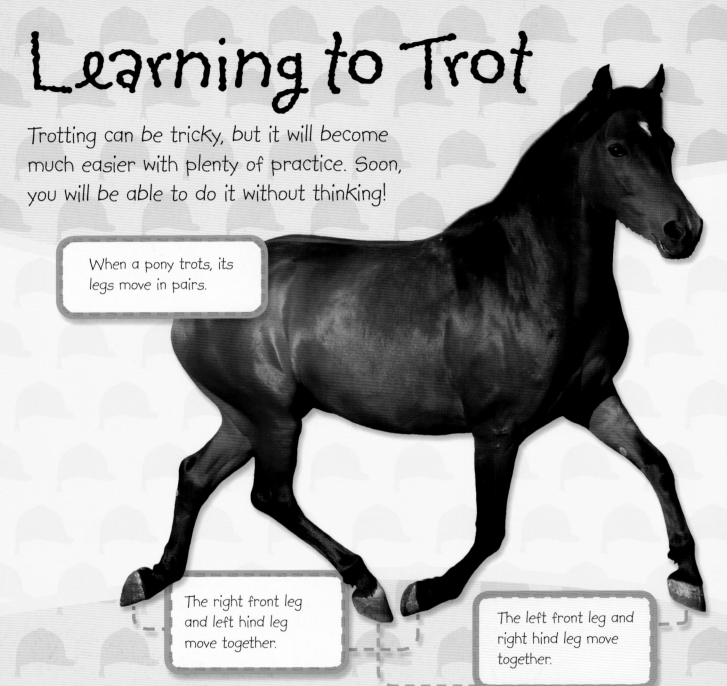

When a pony trots, its legs move in pairs.

The right front leg and left hind leg move together.

The left front leg and right hind leg move together.

Find Your Rhythm
Riding in trot can feel very bumpy. To make it more comfortable, rise up out of the saddle as one pair of the pony's feet hits the ground, and sit down as the opposite pair hits the ground.

Rising to the Trot

It is easier to practice **rising to the trot** with your pony standing still. Stand up in your stirrups and then sit down again gently.

Make sure not to thump down heavily—this will hurt your pony's back.

It's difficult to balance when you first learn to ride. You can try holding onto the saddle for extra support.

Top Tip!

Remember, try not to rise too high out of the saddle, and always sit down gently.

Canter On

When a pony canters, its front and back legs on one side are in front of those on the other. So we say it is "leading" with the right or left leg. If you canter in a circle, or round a corner, the **leading leg** should be on the inside of the curve.

Preparing to Canter

Before you tell your pony to canter, you should be moving in a good, balanced trot. To canter with the right leg leading, shorten your reins, and feel the right one more strongly than the left. Press with your right leg on the girth and with your left leg behind the girth.

Into Canter

Once the pony goes into canter, relax the aids, but keep your reins fairly short. Because the pony's right leg is in front of its left, you will sit slightly askew, with your right shoulder slightly in front of your left shoulder. To canter with the left leg leading, reverse the aids.

This rider is sitting well and has her pony under control.

Sitting to the Canter

The canter is a lovely, swinging pace, but at first you may bounce out of the saddle. Try to sit well down and allow your back relax so you can follow the pony's movement, rather than trying to hold yourself stiffly in position.

When you are cantering, you should be able to feel which leg the pony is leading with—without looking down.

These pictures show how the pony's feet hit the ground when it is cantering.

1. Most of its weight is on its left foreleg.
2. Most of its weight is on its left foreleg and the right hindleg.
3. Another stride begins with both forelegs off the ground.
4. The weight is on the right foreleg and left hind leg.

Top Tip!

If you lean forwards when you are cantering, your pony will think you want it to go faster.

Turning Your Pony

When a pony turns, its front legs and outer hind leg move around its inner hind leg. Its whole body curves around, from head to tail.

Turning Right

When you turn a pony, your hand on the inside of the turn and your leg on the outside of the turn produce the movement.

1. Pull out the right rein to turn the pony's head to the right.

2. Move your left hand to the right, pressing the left rein against its neck.

3. At the same time, press with your left leg behind the girth to push the pony around.

4. Keep your right leg on the girth.

5. Both you and the pony should look in the direction in which you are going.

Turning Left

Your inside leg keeps the pony steady and your outside hand reinforces the action of the inside hand. While the pony is turning, it should not walk forward.

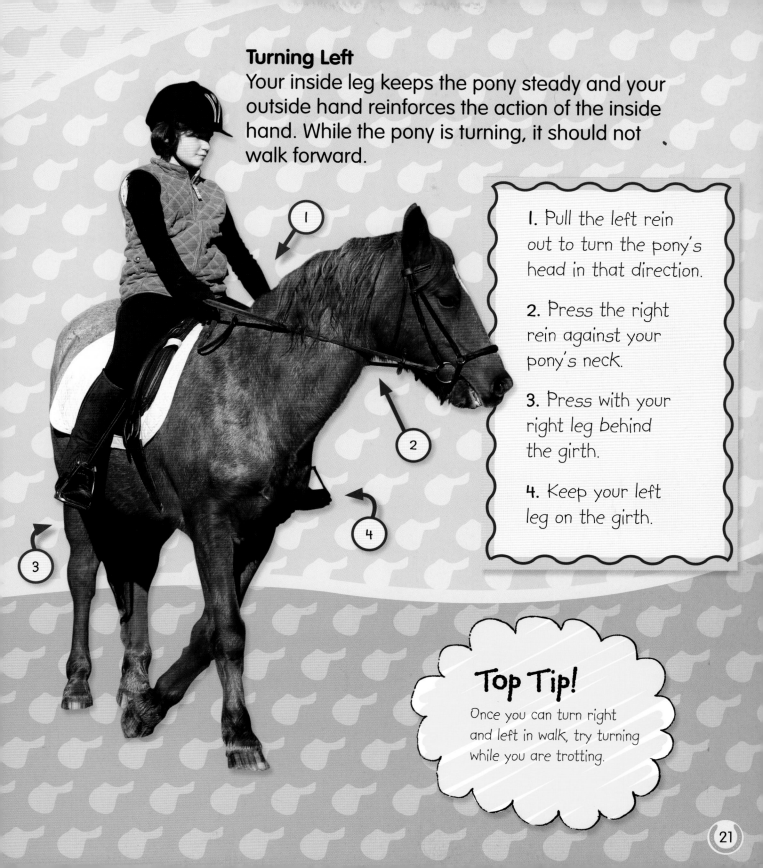

1. Pull the left rein out to turn the pony's head in that direction.

2. Press the right rein against your pony's neck.

3. Press with your right leg behind the girth.

4. Keep your left leg on the girth.

Top Tip!

Once you can turn right and left in walk, try turning while you are trotting.

Ride Western Style

Try riding Western style! First, your legs should be almost straight. Hold the reins in your right hand, separated by your first finger. Tell the pony to go forwards by making a clucking sound, and to stop by saying "Whoa." When you trot Western style, sit down in the saddle instead of rising.

one-ear headstall

Western Bridle
This **bridle** has a loop in the **headpiece** that fits round the pony's ear, and a curb **bit**. A bit is a metal bar that fits in the pony's mouth.

Saddle Up Fact!
Western bridles with bits do not usually have a noseband.

curb bit

Western Saddle

This saddle is much bigger than an English one. The back part, called the cantle, is steeper. It has a horn at the front.

When cowboys are herding cattle, they can tie a cow to the horn with a rope. Cowboy stirrups are made of wood. This is more comfortable for the rider's feet.

cantle

horn

front rigging

wooden stirrup

Riding in walk, the pony can stretch its neck out naturally.

Neck Reining

If you want to turn right, move your right hand over to the right. The right rein will turn the pony's head in the correct direction, and the left rein will press against its neck. This is called neck reining. At the same time, press the pony's side with your left leg. Simply reverse these signals to turn left.

23

Go for a Gallop

The gallop is the pony's fastest pace. Galloping is very exciting, both for the pony and its rider. Before you try to gallop, you must be able to control your pony in canter.

Saddle Up Fact!
A gallop is a four-beat gait. Each hoof hits the ground separately.

Forward Position
When you gallop, you take the weight off the pony's back by going into **"forward position"**— stand up slightly in your stirrups and lean forward. Practice going into forward position with the pony standing still and someone holding it.

Telling a Pony to Gallop

Start in a canter, then shorten your reins and go into forward position. Squeeze with both legs to urge the pony forward. As the pony goes faster, release the pressure from your legs but keep a firm hold of the reins. To slow down, press again with your legs and pull strongly on the reins. Always allow plenty of space in which to stop.

Only gallop with other ponies if you know their riders can control them.

Safety

You should gallop only where it is safe to do so—on a smooth, uphill track, free from stones and potholes. If you are with other ponies, allow plenty of space between them.

Learning to Jump

When you have learned to ride at walk, trot and canter, you can try jumping. You need good balance in the saddle.

Trotting Rails

Your first lessons in learning to jump will be over **trotting poles**. These are poles on the ground, spaced so the pony can walk and trot over them. As you approach the poles, shorten your reins and go into forward position.

Your First Jump

As you approach the jump, shorten your reins and drive the pony forward with your legs. Go into forward position and stay in that position until after the pony has landed, so you don't pull on the reins and hurt its mouth.

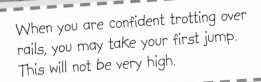

When you are confident trotting over rails, you may take your first jump. This will not be very high.

Get Ready to Jump!

There are four stages to a jump.

1. The Approach

As you approach a jump, you will learn to "see the stride." This means judging how many strides the pony must take before it jumps so it can clear the fence.

2. Takeoff

As the pony takes off, it tucks up its front legs and springs off its hind legs. You must give with your hands to let its neck stretch forward.

3. In the Air

For a brief moment all four legs are off the ground and the pony is "in the air."

4. Landing

The rider stays in forward position until the pony has landed. As it lands, the rider looks forward to the next jump.

Basic Pony Needs

If you keep a pony, you need to give it food, water, shelter, and company. Taking care of it is hard work and takes up a lot of time.

Ponies are unhappy living alone. If you have only one pony, it needs a companion, preferably another pony. However, they can also live with other animals such as sheep or goats.

A Place to Live

You can keep a pony in a field, or partly in a stable and partly in a field. A pony would be unhappy inside all the time because it needs to be able to graze, roll, and roam for at least part of each day. A stable provides shelter from the weather. A pony that lives in a field also needs shelter, such as trees or thick bushes.

Ponies will stand nose to tail in summer so they can swish the flies off each other's faces with their tails.

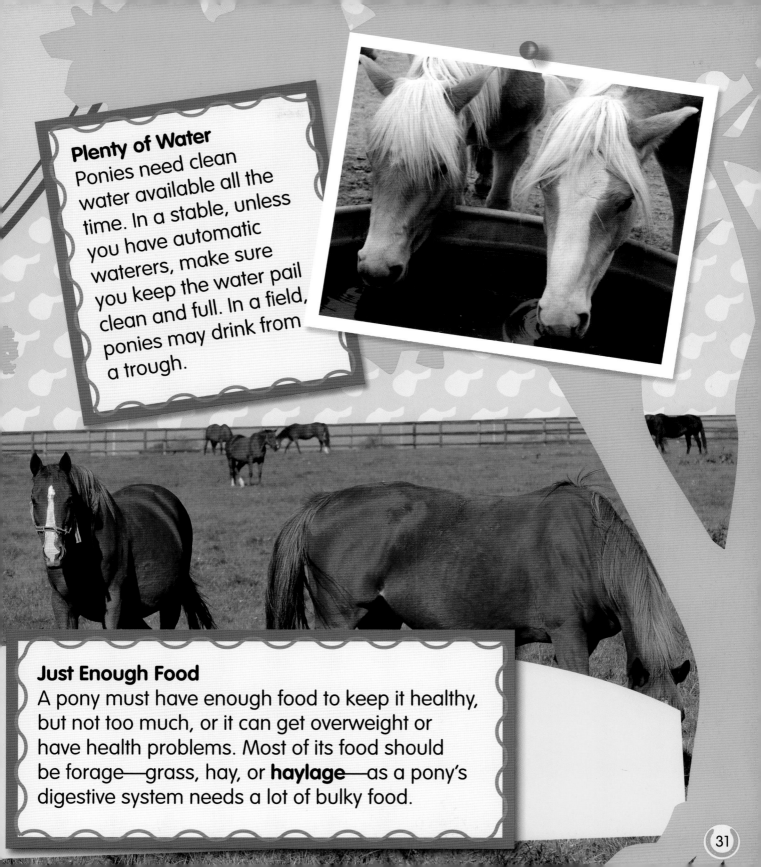

Plenty of Water

Ponies need clean water available all the time. In a stable, unless you have automatic waterers, make sure you keep the water pail clean and full. In a field, ponies may drink from a trough.

Just Enough Food

A pony must have enough food to keep it healthy, but not too much, or it can get overweight or have health problems. Most of its food should be forage—grass, hay, or **haylage**—as a pony's digestive system needs a lot of bulky food.

Out in a Field

A pony's field must have no poisonous plants, be properly fenced, provide shelter, and have a clean water supply. The ground should not be marshy. The best kind of fencing is **post and rail**; the worst is barbwire, especially if it is rusty and sagging.

Looking After the Field

Ponies do not graze **paddocks** evenly. They eat some parts right down to the ground, and leave clumps of long grass in other places. To even out the grazing, leave the paddock empty from time to time, and then let sheep or cattle graze there. Two or three times a year, the field should be "topped"— the tops taken off any weeds.

A poor field

A good field

The field gate should hang properly and open and close easily. It should also be fastened securely so ponies cannot open it.

Clued Up to Care!

Keeping the field free of droppings helps prevent a pony from getting worms.

A trough fills automatically and saves a lot of work carrying water. It must be scrubbed out regularly to keep it clean.

A field shelter protects ponies from bad weather. It has a wide entrance so ponies cannot bully one another when they go in and out.

Poisonous Plants

Ponies should not be put in a field where they can reach any of these plants.

ragwort

yew

bracken

foxglove

rhododendron

belladonna

horsetail

In a Stable

An ideal stable is light and airy without being drafty. It should be big enough for the pony to move around freely.

Traditional stables have half-doors over which ponies can look out.

Sometimes stables are part of a barn, where several horses or ponies can be housed together.

The Building

A small pony can live in a stable measuring 10 by 10 feet. A larger pony needs more space. The floor needs a drainage system to take away liquid waste. Ponies need lots of fresh air, so the top half of the door should be left open. If the top parts of the windows open inward, rain cannot blow in.

Switches and light bulbs should be where the pony cannot reach them.

You need a tying ring to hang a **haynet** and to tie the pony to when grooming.

Bedding and Mucking Out
The stable needs a deep, dry bed for the pony to lie on. The bedding can be **straw**, shavings, baled newspaper or cardstock. You should muck out the stable every day—remove any droppings and wet bedding, and replace it with fresh bedding.

Top Tip!
Manure and dirty bedding can be turned into compost for the garden.

Feeding Time

A pony's natural food is grass. It eats small amounts at a time, but spends many hours each day grazing, so it eats a lot over 24 hours. A pony should also be given extra food if it works hard.

Hard Feed
A hard-working pony needs **hard feed**, such as **coarse mix**, **pony nuts**, maize, and sugar beet, two or three times a day. However, its main food should always be grass or hay (dried grass).

Coarse mix contains a mixture of grains and pony nuts.

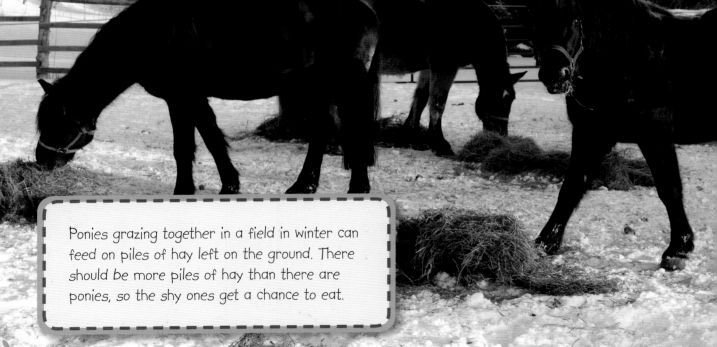

Ponies grazing together in a field in winter can feed on piles of hay left on the ground. There should be more piles of hay than there are ponies, so the shy ones get a chance to eat.

Soaking Hay

Ponies can get coughs from the hay dust. To prevent this, soak the hay in water and then let it drain. You can use a garbage can for this. Be careful, a net full of wet hay is much heavier than a net full of dry hay.

Watering

Ponies need clean, fresh water available all the time. If you do not have automatic waterers in the stable and the field, you must keep the pails filled.

Feeding Routine

It's important to have a timetable for feeding a pony, and to stick to it. If the pony lives in a stable, it will expect breakfast at the same time every morning. It doesn't understand weekends and holidays!

Brush Up!

You should keep your pony clean, but don't over groom a pony that lives outside. Grooming takes the grease out of its coat, which helps keep it warm and dry.

Grooming Kit

A water brush is used damp on the mane and tail to lay the hairs flat.

A hoofpick cleans out the feet.

A rubber curry comb removes dried mud and loose hairs.

Sponges are used for cleaning the eyes and nose, as well as the dock area..

A metal curry comb cleans the body brush.

A dandy brush removes dried mud, sweat, and loose hairs.

A **body brush** removes grease from the coat, and is used to brush the face, mane, and tail.

Grooming a Pony

1. When you groom a pony, start at its neck and work down its shoulder and front leg.

2. Do the other side, then slip off the **headcollar** while you carefully brush its face with the body brush.

3. Then brush its back, tummy, and back legs.

4. Put the headcollar back on. Dampen the sponges, and clean round the eyes and nose with one, and the dock (the area under the tail) with another.

5. Finally, brush out the mane, forelock, and tail with the body brush.

If you need to wash a pony's tail, do it in a pail. Use a horse shampoo, and rinse the tail several times.

Top Tip!

To brush out the tail, hold it in one hand. Let go of a few hairs at a time and brush them downward with the body brush.

Fancy Footcare

It is very important for the pony's health that its feet are kept clean and are trimmed regularly by a **farrier**.

Cleaning Out the Feet

To pick up a pony's foot, slide your hand down its leg, then tug at the fetlock hair and say, "Up." As the pony lifts its foot, slide your hand round to support it. Then, with the other hand, pick the dirt out of the foot with the hoofpick, using it from heel to toe. The feet should be picked out every day.

hoofpick

Trimming the Feet

A pony's hoofs grow all the time, like your fingernails. They need trimming by a farrier every six to eight weeks, whether the pony wears shoes or not.

A neglected hoof in very poor condition

A front hoof wearing a shoe

1. The farrier cuts the clenches (nail ends) and levers off the old shoe.

2. He trims the foot with hoofcutters.

3. He files the foot to make it level.

Shoeing a Pony

If you ride a pony on roads and rough tracks, its feet wear down too quickly, so it needs shoes to protect them. A farrier removes the shoes to trim the feet, then either puts them back on or replaces them.

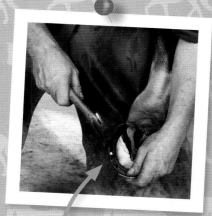

4. The shoe is heated in a furnace, hammered into shape on the anvil, then tried on the hoof. It burns the hoof and makes a lot of smoke, but the pony cannot feel it.

5. The shoe is cooled in a pail of water before being nailed on.

6. The nails go in the underside of the foot and come out at the side.

Weather Watch

In winter and summer, you need to give your pony special care to cope with the weather.

Winter Feeding

Grass has little goodness in it during winter, so ponies need hay even if they live in a field. They may also need some hard feed.

In freezing weather, you have to break the ice on the water trough or bucket.

Clipped ponies, or ponies with fine coats, need to wear a special waterproof rug called a turnout blanket, when out in the field.

Ponies can get sores on their heels and lower legs, called mud fever, in winter. Using special ointments can prevent this.

Straps round the back legs link together to help hold the rug in place.

When a pony works hard in winter, its coat is clipped off to stop it sweating too much and losing condition. There are several different styles of clip. The trace clip (shown here) is the type used most often on ponies. A clipped pony needs to wear a blanket in the stable as well as in the field.

Summer Shade

Ponies out in a field need shade from the hot summer sun. They also need protection from flies. It is best to stable them in the daytime in summer, and put them out at night. Those that are out in the daytime can wear a fly mask (shown here) or even a fly sheet to keep off the flies.

Ponies easily become overweight on rich summer grass. They can also get a painful condition in their feet called **laminitis**. They often have to be kept out of the field for part of each day to stop them eating too much.

Care After Riding

When you have finished your ride, you need to check that all is well with your pony *before* putting it *back* in the field or the stable. If you have worked your pony hard, it will be tired and hungry.

Cooling Down
If you bring a pony in hot and sweating after a ride and leave it standing around, it can get a chill. So always walk the last mile or so home to let it cool down.

Removing the Tack
Back at the stable, take off the pony's bridle and put on its headcollar. Then tie it up, and run the stirrups up the leathers, undo the girth and slide the saddle off the pony's back.

Check the Pony Over
Brush off the saddle patch, and check the legs for any thorns or cuts. Check the feet for stones. If the legs are dry, brush off any mud.

Slide the saddle and the **numnah** back as you lift it off the pony's back to lay the hair flat.

Sponging and Brushing

In hot weather, you can sponge off the saddle patch with water and then dry it with a towel. In winter, especially if the pony is clipped, it must be kept warm. Cover its body with a blanket while you brush it down, folding the blanket back over the shoulders or the quarters to keep it out of the way.

No Gulping!

If the pony is hot and tired after working hard over a long day, just give it a small drink of lukewarm water at first. You can let it drink more later. Then give it a net of hay before its feed to stop it eating too quickly.

Giving water in a shallow container stops the pony from drinking too much at once.

Clued Up to Care!
A pony likes to take its time drinking, lifting its head and then lowering it to drink again.

Health Care

You must look after a pony well to keep it healthy. It needs regular worming and vaccinations as well as exercise, fresh air, and the right amount of food. Once you know what to look for, it is easy to tell the difference between a healthy and a sick pony.

A well-cared-for pony in good health.

Fit and Strong

A healthy pony has a shiny coat, bright eyes, and is interested in everything going on around it. It will always be interested in food!

Sick and Weak

A pony that is sick will have a dull coat. It may have dull eyes, a sad expression, and may be thin, with its ribs sticking out.

An old, thin pony like this may need its teeth checked by a dentist.

Colic

Colic is a pain in a pony's stomach. It can be serious, and you need to call the vet. Ponies with colic keep lying down to roll, then standing up again. They may also turn round and snatch at their stomach with their teeth.

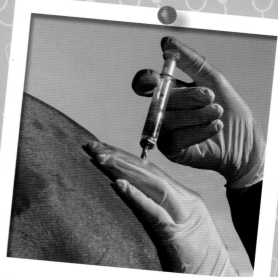

Ponies need a vaccination each year to protect them from equine flu and tetanus.

A pony needs worming regularly. Medicine is mixed into its feed, or squirted onto its tongue. Worming kills parasites that live in the pony's intestines.

Laminitis

Usually caused by overeating, especially of spring and summer grass, laminitis gives a pony hot, painful feet, and makes it lame. A pony with laminitis often stands leaning back on its heels to try to take the weight off its toes.

Joining a Riding Club

Whether or not you have your own pony, you can have fun joining a riding club or a branch of The Pony Club. You will meet other children and their ponies, and learn a lot about riding and pony care.

The Pony Club
In United States Pony Club (U.S.P.C.), a program for youths, teaches riding, mounted sports, and the care of horses and ponies. There are Pony Club centers across the United States, so it should be easy to find one in your neighborhood. Other countries have their own versions of The Pony Club, too.

This young rider is wearing a Pony Club tie as part of her riding outfit.

Riding clubs often have their own premises, which will have a riding ring and jumps for you to practice going over.

Going to Meetings

Some branches of The Pony Club and some riding clubs hold meetings at other riding schools, which means you can go along even if you don't have your own pony. They will let you handle and ride one of their ponies.

Indoor School

These riding club members are lucky to have the use of an indoor school for their lessons. This means that they can ride and do exercises in the saddle whatever the weather.

When you go to a meeting, an instructor will help you with your riding, and answer questions about pony care.

Going to Meetings

You may be lucky enough to live near the meeting place of your club, and be able to ride there. If not, you will need transport for your pony.

Transport

Ponies can travel in either a **horse truck** or a horse trailer. Sometimes you can share transport with a friend.

This truck can carry several horses or ponies.

This trailer can be pulled by a car.

Trailer Travel

A pony can travel in a two-horse trailer, like this one, either with or without the central partition in place. Some trailers also have side ramps, so you can lead the pony out forward—otherwise you have to back it down the ramp to unload it.

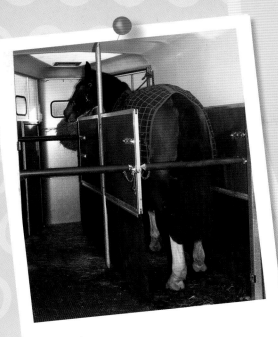

Safety
Ponies need to be **cross-tied** (tied on both sides) when they are traveling in a horsetruck or trailer to stop them from trying to move around.

Into the Trailer
When you lead a pony into a horse truck or trailer, walk confidently straight up the ramp.

This horse is wearing a travel blanket, boots and a tail wrap.

Protective Clothing
When a pony travels in a horse truck or trailer, it needs **travel boots** to protect its legs from knocks, and a tail wrap to prevent any rubbing. If you are not going far, it can travel with its **tack** on.

Learning More

When you go to meetings of The Pony Club or your riding club, you will learn a lot about ponies, such as how to keep your pony fit and healthy.

Top Tip!

Learn the points of a horse so you know a forelock from a **fetlock**!

Points of a Horse
It's important to know the correct names of the different parts of a pony's anatomy. Then you will know what people are talking about when they refer to, for example, its hock.

forelock

ear

crest

withers

back

loins

tail

cheek

nose

thigh

shoulder

chest

belly

knee

hoof

hock

fetlock

Pony Fitness

You can help a pony to get fit by gradually increasing the amount of exercise it does, cutting down its grazing, and giving it more hard feed.

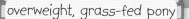

overweight, grass-fed pony

fit pony

How to Lead a Pony

Lead your pony on its left side, with your right hand near its head and your left hand at the end of the line. Then, if needed, you can let go with your right hand and bring the pony around with your left hand.

Approaching a Strange Pony

Walk toward the pony's head from one side. Speak to it, let it sniff your closed fist and pat it on the neck. That way the pony knows that you are a friend.

Improving Your Riding

Some of your riding club meetings will show you exercises to improve your riding and your confidence in the saddle. Some of these can be done while the horse is led on a long line that is attached to a special headcollar. This is called **longeing**.

Riding Without Stirrups

You can ride with your stirrups crossed over your saddle to help improve your seat in the saddle and your balance. If you feel insecure, hold on to the front of the saddle.

Riding Without Lines

Knotting your lines and riding without them will also improve your balance when riding. The person holding the longe line will control the pony.

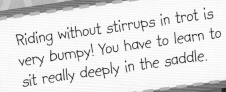

Riding without stirrups in trot is very bumpy! You have to learn to sit really deeply in the saddle.

Exercises in the Saddle

There are lots of exercises you can do while you are sitting on a pony as long as someone is holding it for you. The exercises will make you supple and give you more confidence.

Hold your arms out and twist around to each side from your waist.

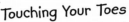

Touching Your Toes

Lift your right hand up in the air then bend down to touch your left foot. Straighten up, then repeat the exercise with your left hand touching your right foot.

Lying Back

Lie back until your head touches the pony's back. Try to sit up again without holding on to the saddle, but if you can't, then pull yourself up using the front of the saddle.

Working Harder

As your riding improves, you will learn more advanced exercises, and also how to handle problem ponies.

Making Your Pony Move

Some ponies don't want to go forward. To encourage your pony, shorten the reins, squeeze hard with your legs and say firmly, "Walk on." If it still doesn't move, you can use a stick just behind the girth (the strap under the horse's belly) to reinforce your leg aid.

Moving too Quickly

Some ponies want to set off at great speed, especially when they canter. First of all, never lean forward, as this will make the pony think you want it to go faster. Keep your reins short and sit down in the saddle. If possible, try to ride the pony round in a circle to slow it down, but don't turn it too fast or it could fall over.

Working as a Pair

Riding around side by side with another pony is a good exercise in control. There are classes for riding in pairs at shows, and it's fun to do, though much more difficult than it looks. The ponies' heads should be level, and remember that when you turn, the pony on the outside has to move faster than the one on the inside.

Meet Up Fact!
Ponies ridden side by side may want to race each other if they canter.

When riding as a pair, it's easier if the larger pony is on the outer side of the smaller one.

Pony Club Camp

Every summer, branches of The Pony Club and some riding clubs go away to summer camp. It's a chance to have lots of fun with your friends and their ponies.

At the Camp
You will probably sleep in a tent, and your pony will be turned out with the others in a field. You will have to take care of your pony yourself, and also help with cooking meals and keeping the camp tidy.

These ponies have had their morning ride and are resting before a class in the school later on.

My Pony Club Summer Camp Diary

7 a.m. I crawled out of my sleeping bag, got dressed, and went out to feed the ponies. It's a bright, sunny day—hooray!

7:30 a.m. Our leader built a fire and cooked eggs over it. We had a delicious breakfast.

8:30 a.m. After doing the dishes, we groomed and tacked up the ponies.

9 a.m. We set off on a long ride. Luckily, our camp was near the ocean, so we rode along the beach. We tried riding in the shallow water, but some of the ponies didn't want to go in!

12:30 p.m. We returned to camp, brushed the ponies over and turned them out in the field.

1 p.m. Picnic time! We all ate lunch on the grass.

2 p.m. After lunch, we went into the indoor school for a talk about pony care and feeding by one of The Pony Club officials. I had no idea there was so much to learn!

5 p.m. Dinnertime, with ice cream for dessert. Then we cleaned the tack.

7 p.m. We checked the ponies one last time and then went back to our tents and got ready to go to sleep. It was supposed to be lights out at 8 p.m., but I was so tired, I was asleep long before that!

Fun at Camp

You will have a great time away at camp, with nothing but ponies to think about. You will spend your whole day riding them and caring for them.

Group Sessions
You may have group classes with other riders in a field or an outdoor school. These may be lessons in basic riding, or more advanced skills, such as jumping.

Riding for a Day
You may go out on a whole day's ride, taking a lunch box with you. Your pony may wear a headcollar over its bridle, so you can remove its bit and allow it to graze at lunchtime. You will also stop to let it drink when you are near water.

Aftercare

After riding, you will need to take water and food to your pony before you have your own meal. If it is put in a stable, it will also need hay.

Cleaning the Tack

To make this task more fun, do it with your friends. First, clean off the grease and any mud with a damp sponge, then rub in saddle soap. Wet the soap, not the sponge, to avoid getting too much foam.

At the end of the day's riding you will need to clean the pony's tack (its saddle and bridle).

Top Tip!

If you keep your tack clean and supple, it will last for many years.

Team Games

Your riding club or branch of The Pony Club may have a team that competes in games events. If you have a pony that can gallop and turn quickly, and you are good at jumping on and off, you may be able to join the team.

Old Sock Race
In this race, each competitor collects a rolled up sock, gallops down the field and drops it into a pail. The first team to get all their socks in the pail wins.

Tack Store Race
Here each member of the team has to pick up an item of tack or grooming equipment, gallop down the field and drop them into a box held by another member.

Five Mug Race
The first rider in each team gallops halfway down the field, picks up a mug from a stack upturned on a post, then gallops down the rest of the field to put the mug on top of another post. They then gallop back to the start, and when they get there the second rider sets off. The first team to move all the cups from the first post to the second wins.

Tire Race
In this event a pair of riders races down the field. One jumps off while the other holds her pony, climbs through a tire, then remounts, and the pair gallop back to the start. The first rider dismounts and a third takes her place, the pair gallop off again, and the new rider climbs through the tire. This goes on until everyone has taken a turn, and the team to finish first wins.

Stepping Stone Dash
In this race, riders have to vault off their ponies, run along a row of upturned pails, then vault back on again and gallop back to the start.

Preparing Your Pony

When you enter your pony in a competition, it must look its best—clean and well groomed—to help you and your pony do the best you can.

You can trim the long hair on a pony's fetlocks and mane. To trim the tail, ask someone to hold it out slightly, so you can trim it neatly and level.

Grooming

To get your pony's coat gleaming, you need to groom it well with a body brush. Then give it a final polish with the stable rubber to remove dust and loose hairs.

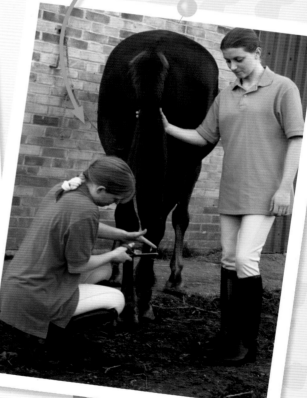

Quarter Marks

Patterns made on the pony's quarters using a comb, or a stencil and a damp water brush, are called quarter marks. Brush or comb the hair in different directions to create the effect.

Braiding the Mane and Tail

You can braid the top of the tail to make it look tidy. Manes can be divided into sections, which are braided, folded under, and stitched into place.

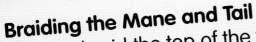

Top Tip!

It is easier to braid the mane if you dampen the sections first.

You should take care of your pony's tack, so that it lasts a long time.

Cleaning the Tack

Clean the tack (the saddle and bridle) every time you use it, and give it a good clean before a competition. Rub saddle soap into the leather with a damp sponge until the tack is soft. Wash the bit and stirrup irons carefully to get rid of all the dirt, then rub them dry until they gleam.

At the Show

If you are going to ride in a show, make sure that you look as tidy and clean as your pony. When you're at a show, rest your pony between classes. Let it graze, and give it a drink of water.

hard hat

stock

gloves

riding jacket

jodhpurs

riding boots

Riding clothes

At a show, you need to wear proper riding clothes— jodhpurs with riding boots, a stock or tie and shirt, a riding jacket, gloves, and your hard hat. Your clothes should be clean and tidy, and your boots must be well polished.

If you are competing in jumping classes, you will need to wear a body protector. This protects your back from injury in case you fall off.

Arriving

Try to arrive at a show with plenty of time to spare. Register for your class then, while you are waiting to be called, make sure your pony is clean, tidy, and comfortable.

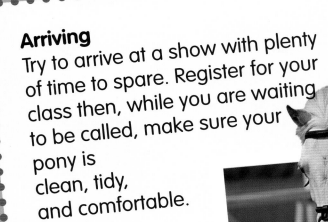

If you're in a jumping class, you will be able to jump over a few practice rails while you wait.

In the Collecting Ring

The collecting ring is a small ring near the entrance to the main ring, where competitors wait until it is time for their class. You may want to practice your trot and canter, but don't work the pony too hard. You don't want it to be sweating when you enter the ring.

Leadline Class

If you are young and new to riding, your first **showing** class may well be on a leadline. A parent or another adult will lead the pony around while you ride as well as you can.

Correct Dress

In a leadline class, both the handler and the rider have to wear the right clothes. For men, this is a suit, a tie, gloves and a hat; for women, this is a skirt, jacket, hat, and gloves.

This pony, its rider, and handler all look very smart.

In the Ring

The leadline competitors walk, then trot, around the ring together. The judge then calls them in to line up, and each does an **individual show**, such as trotting a circle in each direction.

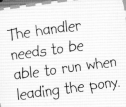

The handler needs to be able to run when leading the pony.

Choosing the Winner

When everyone has done their show, the ponies walk around again. Then, they line up in winning order—first, second, third, and so on. The first four or five receive a ribbon.

First Riding and Showing Classes

Many shows have a special class for young riders who are competing in a show for the first time off the leadline.

First Riding Classes

These classes are for young riders, but this time you ride alone. The ponies go around together in both walk and trot, and then line up, as in the leadline class. The judge examines the ponies one at a time, and you each do an individual show. In this class you may canter, as well as walk and trot, in your show.

walk

trot

canter

Categories of Showing Class

Height	Rider Age
Up to 12.2 hh (50 inches)	Up to 13 years
12.2 hh to 13.2 hh (54 inches)	Up to 15 years
13.2 hh to 14.2 hh (59 inches)	Up to 17 years

Showing Classes

Similar to the first riding classes, the showing classes allow you to canter around the ring together, as well as walk and trot. You will also have to dismount, remove your pony's saddle, and walk and trot it out to show the judge how well your pony moves.

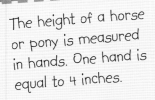

The height of a horse or pony is measured in hands. One hand is equal to 4 inches.

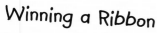

Winning a Ribbon

If you win a ribbon, the judge attaches it to the pony's bridle, or to the string of your number. You will canter around the ring in a lap of honor, in the order of judging. When the spectators clap, be sure you have control of your pony, or it may get over excited.

Leading an unridden horse or pony around a show ring is called showing **in hand**.

Show Jumping

These classes combine the skills needed for both showing classes and show jumping.

In the Ring
A show jumping pony is expected to do all the things a show pony does, as well as gallop and jump. In Phase One, each competitor goes around the jumping course in turn. In Phase Two, the whole class goes around the ring together in walk, trot, and canter. Finally, the ponies gallop round the ring one at a time.

It's Showtime!
A score is given for each phase. The scores are added together to find the winner.

The course might include jumps such as these rails. The jumps won't be too high.

Show Jumping

This sport involves riding around a course and going over many different types of jumps. The jumps are colored and have different distances between them.

Preparing to Jump

You can walk around a show jumping course before the class and work out how many strides you need to take when approaching each jump. The jumps are numbered to help you know your way around. Competitors jump the course one at a time.

The Scoring System
Each competitor collects **faults** for knocking down jumps, refusing to jump them, missing one or going over the time limit. The rider with the smallest number of faults wins.

Types of Jumps

Show jumping rings contain "spread" jumps such as an oxer, and "uprights" such as a wall. The "bricks" are wooden blocks that are easy to knock down without injuring the pony.

Oxer

Crossed Rails

Wall

Pony Show Games

Entering games classes is lots of fun. Many of them are races, and you need a speedy pony that will turn and stop when and where you want it to. It is useful to be able to vault onto your pony to save time.

With lots of practice, you can vault onto a pony while it's moving.

Bending Race
This race needs a well trained pony. You have to weave your way along a line of upright poles, turn at the end, then weave your way back again.

Potato Race

In this race, you have to pick up a potato, gallop down the field, and then put it in a pail. You then go back for the next potato, and the person who gets all their potatoes in the pail first is the winner.

Sack Race

In this race, you canter down the field, get off your pony, and climb into a sack. Then, leading your pony, you get back to the start as fast as you can. Most people jump along, holding the pony with one hand, and the sack with the other.

Egg and Spoon Race

Carrying an egg on a spoon while running as fast as you can and leading your pony is not easy. The eggs aren't real ones, but if you do drop one, you have to stop and pick it up again.

Handy Pony Class

For the handy pony, or handy ranch, class you need an obedient, calm, well-behaved pony. In this class, you have to do all kinds of unusual tasks while riding

A task may involve walking or trotting over a number of rails laid on the ground.

Your pony needs to be well behaved while you jump and lead it at the same time as walking along a row of upturned pots.

You might have to dismount, pick something up, then mount again, and take the object to another part of the ring.

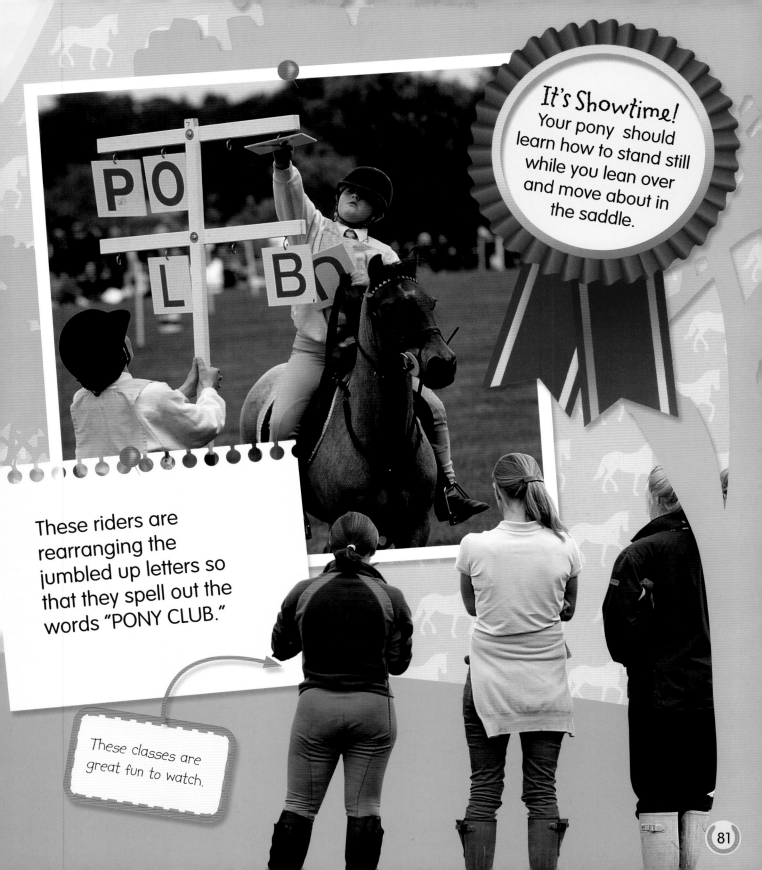

It's Showtime!
Your pony should learn how to stand still while you lean over and move about in the saddle.

These riders are rearranging the jumbled up letters so that they spell out the words "PONY CLUB."

These classes are great fun to watch.

Dress Up Class

This is a lot of fun! In a dress up class, you and your pony wear a costume. You are characters, so you need to plan your outfits, and you may need some help in making it. The best costume wins.

Spots Before Your Eyes
This rider has made her pony match her costume by painting spots on it. If you do this, only use washable water based paint so you can wash it off again.

This young rider has used pink paint on the pony's mane and tail and given it a paper horn to look like a unicorn!

Western Dress!

Clothing worn for Western riding events—such as reining, cutting, and rodeo—consists of jeans, cowboy boots, a cowboy hat, a long sleeved shirt, and protective leather leggings called chaps. Bright colors and fancy patterns are popular.

You could wear a Santa suit or an elf costume. Then turn your pony into Rudolph the Red Nosed Reindeer.

Rudolph Costume

Fix fake antlers to your pony's bridle and paint its nose red with water based paint. Then twist tinsel around the bridle, draping it over the pony's neck.

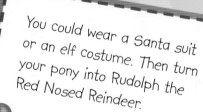

Dressage and Eventing

Dressage and eventing are competitions for experienced riders. In dressage, your pony has to perform precise movements and paces.

The Dressage Arena
A dressage arena has a low fence round it and letters along the sides. Most arenas measure 130 feet by 65 feet, but for some international competitions, they are 195 feet by 65 feet.

Markers around an arena
130 by 65 feet

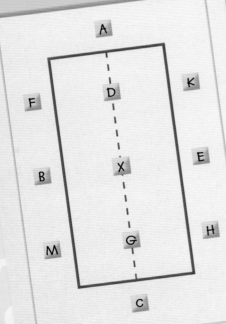

You have to learn the test first—although in some **novice** tests, it may be read out to you. For example, you might walk into the arena at A, trot to C, canter from C to F, walk from F to E, and so on.

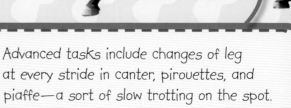

Advanced tasks include changes of leg at every stride in canter, pirouettes, and piaffe—a sort of slow trotting on the spot.

Eventing

This sport involves dressage, cross-country and show jumping. In the cross-country section, you ride a course of difficult jumps within a set time. The course usually involves jumping into and out of a lake.

Cross Country

To ride "cross-country" means galloping over a course of jumps set out in wooded areas. You have to be an experienced rider, with a bold, brave horse or pony.

Hunter Trials

These are jumping competitions ridden across fields and through woods, for both horses and ponies. You may also have to open and close gates. There is usually a set time in which the course has to be completed.

Horse and Pony Breeds

You can look up all your favorite horse and pony breeds in this section! Here is a table of contents to help you find them.

Irish Sport Horse	101
Kiso	108
Konik	97
Landais	90
Lipizzaner	88
Mangalarga Marchador	105
Mecklenburg	96
Morgan	100
Mustang	103
National Show Horse	91
Nokota	109
Noriker	107
Oldenburger	106
Orlov Trotter	102
Palomino	104
Paso Fino	95
Percheron	99
Peruvian Paso	106
Pinto	108
Quarter Horse	94
Quarter Pony	101
Rhinelander	90
Selle Francais	94
Shetland Pony	95
Shire Horse	98
Suffolk	105
Tennessee Walking Horse	89
Thoroughbred	107
Trakehner	100
Welsh Cob	103
Welsh Mountain Pony	98
Zemaitukas	99

Appaloosa

Height: 14 to 16 hands
Color: Spotted coat on a variety of base colors
Comes from: USA

Highly popular among Native American tribes, this breed has been seen in many Western movies.

Barb

Height: 13.3 to 14.1 hands
Color: Mainly gray but also bay, black, chestnut, or brown
Comes from: Barbary Coast, North Africa

A desert horse with strong front legs and a short back, with loads of energy and stamina.

Lipizzaner

Height: 16 hands
Color: Gray, rarely bay or black
Comes from: Austria, Slovenia, and Croatia

Lipizzaners are famous as the "dancing white horses" of Vienna, where they perform in the Spanish Riding School.

Tennessee walking horse

Height: 15.2 hands

Color: Black, bay, chestnut, palomino, buckskin roan, and often spotted patterns

Comes from: USA

Sometimes called "plantation walkers" as they carried their owners across their southern plantations. They have a very comfortable stride.

Galiceno

Height: 12 to 13.2 hands

Color: Bay, black, or chestnut

Comes from: Mexico

Children that are learning to ride or jump can try this breed as it is very friendly and gentle!

Caspian

Height: 12 hands

Color: All solid colors are common

Comes from: Iran

A kind and intelligent breed that is a good jumper despite its small size. It is a very ancient breed and quite rare.

Australian Pony

Height: 11 to 14 hands
Color: Bay, gray, chestnut, or black
Comes from: Australia

This is a great show pony with influences from the Welsh pony and Arab.

Rhinelander

Height: 16.2 hands and over
Color: Any color, but commonly chestnut
Comes from: Germany

These horses are primarily bred for dressage and show jumping. They are also handsome and athletic.

Landais

Height: 13.1 hands
Color: Bay, chestnut, black, or brown
Comes from: Southwest France

They are commonly used as a children's pony because they are intelligent and friendly.

National Show Horse

Height: 14 to 16.2 hands
Color: Bay, gray, chestnut, black, pinto, or palomino
Comes from: USA

A versatile breed, they can be used for saddle seat riding, show jumping, endurance, dressage, or Western riding.

Dole

Height: 14 to 15 hands
Color: Bay, brown, or black
Comes from: Norway

Influences from thoroughbred horses have made the dole much lighter and a good riding horse with a lovely trot.

Clydesdale

Height: 16 to 18 hands
Color: Mostly bay, sometimes with large white markings
Comes from: Scotland

These tall and heavy horses were originally used for farming but can also be kept for riding.

Haflinger

Height: 13 to 15 hands
Color: Chestnut with a lighter mane and tail
Comes from: Austria and northern Italy
These smart and gentle horses are sometimes used for theraputic riding, to help children with disabilities.

Dutch Heavy Draft

Height: 16 hands
Color: Chestnut, bay, black, or gray
Comes from: The Netherlands
This is the heaviest of the Dutch draft breeds. These strong and willing horses often lead long work lives.

American Paint Horse

Height: 14.2 to 16.2 hands
Color: Black, gray, chestnut, or bay patches on a white background
Comes from: USA
This strong horse belongs to a group called "stock horses," which are used for herding cattle in the USA.

Ardennes

Height: 15 to 16 hands
Color: Bay, roan, or chestnut, black is not allowed
Comes from: France, Belgium, and Luxemburg
This is a draft horse breed that is used on farms for its strength and power.

Icelandic

Height: 13 to 14 hands
Color: Chestnut, bay, black, palomino, pinto, or roan
Comes from: Iceland
Friendly and easy to handle, but also enthusiastic and self-assured.

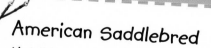

American Saddlebred

Height: 15 to 16 hands
Color: All colors, but mostly chestnut
Comes from: Kentucky, USA
Sometimes known as the "peacock" of the horse show world, this horse is great for driving, riding, and dressage.

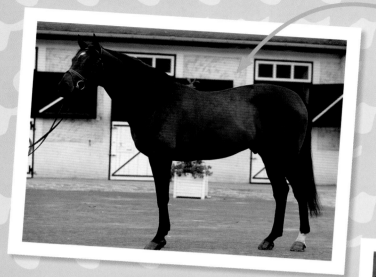

Selle Francais
Height: 16.2 to 17 hands
Color: Bay and chestnut
Comes from: France

These tall and strong horses are very popular for show jumping, but are also seen in dressage and eventing.

Quarter Horse
Height: 14 to 16 hands
Color: Nearly all colors, mostly sorrel
Comes from: USA

Very good at sprinting short distances.

Andalusian
Height: 15.2 hands
Color: Mostly gray
Comes from: Iberican peninsula, Spain

Known for their intelligence, sensitivity, and obedience.

Paso Fino

Height: 14 hands
Color: Most solid colors
Comes from: Puerto Rico

This breed is noted for its agility, intelligence, and hardiness. Its name means "fine walk."

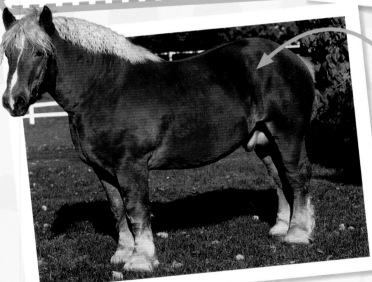

Breton

Height: 15 to 16 hands
Color: Chestnut with lighter mane and tail, bay, roan, or gray
Comes from: France

A quiet, careful horse which is often used to work in vineyards.

Shetland Pony

Height: Up to 10.2 hands
Color: All colors
Comes from: Shetland Islands, UK

These little ponies are very strong for their size and can carry a full grown adult.

Mecklenburg

Height: 15.2 to 17 hands
Color: Chestnut, bay, black, or gray
Comes from: Germany

The Mecklenburg was bred to be a "general" horse so it could be used in the army and on farms.

Arab

Height: 14 to 15 hands
Color: All solid colors except palomino
Comes from: Arabian Peninsula

Highly recognizable for its distinctive head shape and high tailcarriage, this is one of the oldest and most popular horse breeds in the world.

Friesian

Height: 15 hands
Color: Black
Comes from: The Netherlands

This compact horse with great presence is used for dressage and to pull carriages. It is also often used for movies.

Konik

Height: 13 hands
Color: Mouse dun with black markings and stripe along the back
Comes from: Poland

Konik means "small horse" and these tough little creatures are more horse than pony. They are used for farm work and are friendly and gentle.

Cleveland Bay

Height: 16 to 16.2 hands
Color: Bay with a black mane
Comes from: England, UK

These well muscled horses are used for driving and make good riding horses. They also pull carriages in English royal processions.

Fjord

Height: 13 to 14 hands
Color: Dun coat with primitive markings
Comes from: Norway

These horses have a distinct creamy dun coat that grows thick and fluffy in the winter. This breed is one of the oldest in the world.

Shire Horse

Height: 16 to 17 hands
Color: Black, bay, gray, or roan
Comes from: England, UK

These are the largest and tallest horses in the world, the record being 21 hands set by "Mammoth" in 1848.

French Trotter

Height: 16.2 hands
Color: Chestnut, bay, or brown
Comes from: Normandy, France

Bred especially for trotting races in the 19th century.

Welsh Mountain Pony

Height: 12 hands
Color: All solid colors
Comes from: Wales, UK

This breed has roamed the Welsh hills for over a thousand years.

Zemaitukas

Height: 12.2 to 14 hands
Color: Dun color with a dark stripe from mane to tail
Comes from: Lithuania

This is a very old breed and is similar to the Konik. It was used as a war horse and is very quick.

Connemara

Height: Up to 14.2 hands
Color: Black, bay, gray, brown, dun, with occasional roans and chestnuts
Comes from: Ireland

Connemaras were mainly used to carry things such as corn, potatoes, and seaweed to market. They are intelligent and very good at jumping.

Percheron

Height: 16.1 to 16.3 hands
Color: Gray or black
Comes from: France

The Percheron is very elegant for a heavy breed and is found in great numbers not just in France but all over Britain, America, and Canada.

Morgan

Height: 14.2 hands

Color: A variety of colors although most commonly bay, black, or chestnut

Comes from: USA

In 1961, the Morgan horse was named the official state animal of Vermont, and in 1970 the official state horse of Massachusetts.

Fell

Height: 14 hands

Color: Black, dark brown, dark bay, and sometimes gray or dun

Comes from: England, UK

With its wavy mane and tail, this breed is now used as a riding pony.

Trakehner

Height: Up to 17 hands

Color: Chestnut, bay, black, or gray

Comes from: Germany

Renowned for their grace, power, and manner. This breed is very popular in Germany.

Quarter Pony

Height: Up to 14.2 hands
Color: Any color or combination of colors
Comes from: USA

Quarter ponies are often used in Western riding.

Exmoor

Height: 12.3 hands
Color: Black with brown "points" and a lighter colored muzzle
Comes from: England, UK

Exmoor ponies run wild in the moorlands of Devon, UK, and, if taken from the moors early, make very good horses for young people.

Irish Sport Horse

Height: 15 to 17 hands
Color: Any solid color
Comes from: Ireland

This popular riding and competition horse is calm, but lively when needed, and is very tough.

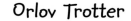

Orlov Trotter

Height: Up to 17 hands
Color: Mostly gray
Comes from: Russia

Named after Count Alexius Orlov who bred five other breeds together to produce the Orlov.

Azteca

Height: 15 hands
Color: Any solid color
Comes from: Mexico

This breed combines athletic ability with good temperament to make strong horses with sloping shoulders.

Basuto Pony

Height: Up to 14.2 hands
Color: Bay, chestnut, gray, or brown
Comes from: South Africa

The Basuto is as tough as a wild horse. It will run on difficult terrain because of its very hard hoofs where other horses would hesitate to walk.

Dartmoor Pony

Height: 12.2 hands
Color: Bay, brown, black, gray, chestnut, or roan
Comes from: Dartmoor, UK

Although several hundred of these horses still live freely in Dartmoor National Park, UK, they are also used for riding.

Welsh Cob

Height: 15 hands
Color: All colors seen
Comes from: Wales, UK

These stout horses are known for their good temperament, hardiness, and free moving gait.

Mustang

Height: 13.1 to 15 hands
Color: A variety of colors, but commonly found in bay, chestnut, black, and gray
Comes from: North America

The mustang is a free roaming feral horse and is a protected breed.

Palomino

Height: 14 to 17 hands
Color: A gold coat and white mane and tail
Comes from: Unknown

Due to their unusual color, Palominos are much sought after as parade horses.

Boulonnais

Height: 16 to 17 hands
Color: Black, bay, red roan, blue roan, or dappled gray
Comes from: France

Strong and elegant horses, used in France to bring fresh fish and oysters to Paris. Every two years in Boulogne they have a race called the "The Fish Route" to commemorate the horses.

Camargue

Height: 13 to 14 hands
Color: Gray only
Comes from: Camargue area, southern France

These beautiful wild horses have lived freely in the Camargue area for possibly thousands of years. They are sometimes tamed by Camargue "cowboys."

Mangalarga Marchador

Height: 14.2 to 16 hands
Color: All colors and markings
Comes from: Brazil
Known for their beauty, intelligence, and good disposition.

Suffolk

Height: 16 hands
Color: Chestnut
Comes from: England, UK
These horses are always chestnut in color and, unlike most heavy breeds, have a very light feather on their feet.

Hanoverian

Height: 15.3 to 17 hands
Color: Chestnut, bay, brown, or black
Comes from: Germany
Very successful horses in show jumping, these German warmbloods are strong, elegant, and robost.

Oldenburger

Height: 16 to 17.2 hands
Color: Variety of colors, but are usually black, brown, or gray
Comes from: Germany

Particularly suitable for dressage and jumping.

Peruvian Paso

Height: 14.1 to 15.2 hands
Color: Chestnut, black, bay, brown, buckskin, palomino, gray, roan, or dun
Comes from: Peru

Loved all over the world for their good temperament and active, flashy paces.

Anglo-Norman

Height: 15.2 to 17 hands
Color: Usually gray, sometimes black, bay, or chestnut
Comes from: France

The Anglo-Norman was developed in the 19th century by crossing horses from France with the English thoroughbred.

Groningen

Height: 15.3 to 16.1
Color: Black or bay
Comes from: The Netherlands

This is a great family horse that is easy to keep and enjoyable to ride.

Thoroughbred

Height: 15.2 to 17 hands
Color: Bay, brown, chestnut, black, or gray
Comes from: England, UK

These agile, fast, and spirited horses are great at racing.

Noriker

Height: Up to 15 hands
Color: Roan, bay, black, or chestnut, sometimes spotted
Comes from: Austria

Also known as Norico-Pinzgauer, this breed originated from the tops of the highest mountains in Austria.

Pinto

Height: 14.2 to 16 hands

Color: A coat color that consists of large patches of white and any other color

Comes from: USA

Various cultures throughout history have selectively bred for pinto patterns.

Kiso

Height: 13 hands

Color: All colors

Comes from: Japan

The Kiso comes from a Japanese mountain region and is small and hardy.

German Riding Pony

Height: 13 to 14 hands

Color: All colors

Comes from: Germany

These ponies are great for learning to ride and jump, and are very popular in Germany.

Auxois

Height: 15.2 to 16.2 hands
Color: Chestnut, bay, or roan
Comes from: France

A handsome, powerful draft horse with a massive body, but a calm and gentle temperament.

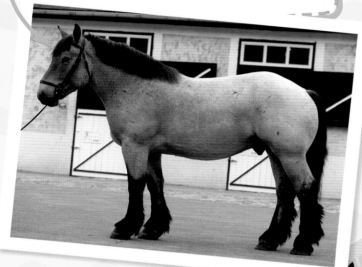

Nokota

Height: Around 14 hands
Color: All colors, but commonly roan
Comes from: USA

These horses are very similar to Mustang and ranching horses. They take their name from North Dakota, USA.

Gypsy Vanner

Height: 14.2 to 15.2 hands
Color: All varieties of color and marking
Comes from: Europe

An old breed used by travelers, these beautifully marked horses are becoming popular all over the world.

Glossary

Aids The signals you give to your pony with your hands, legs, body weight, and voice to tell it what you want it to do.

Bit A metal bar that goes in the pony's mouth. It is part of the bridle.

Body brush A short bristled brush used for removing dirt and grease from a pony's coat.

Bridle The headgear a pony wears when it is being ridden.

Clipped When a pony's winter coat has been removed to stop it from sweating when working hard.

Coarse mix A mixture of feed grains such as maize, barley, dried peas, and beans.

Cross-tied When a pony is tied up in a horse truck or trailer with a rope on each side so it cannot turn around.

Dressage A competition in which a horse or pony has to carry out precise actions and paces.

Farrier Someone who trims horses' feet and shoes them.

Faults Penalty points gained in jumping competitions.

Fetlocks The lowest joints in a horse's or pony's legs, just above the hooves.

Forward position Leaning forward out of the saddle with your weight on the stirrups. This is used when you are galloping and jumping.

Girth The broad strap that goes around a pony's tummy to hold the saddle in place.

Hard feed Concentrated cereals fed to a horse or pony in small quantities.

Haylage Grass which is cut and partly dried before being packed in bales.

Haynet Mesh bag in which hay is fed.

Headcollar Equipment that fits on a pony's head so you can lead it and tie it up.

Headpiece The part of the bridle that fits over the top of the pony's head.

Horse truck A truck in which horses or ponies are transported.

In-hand Leading an unridden horse or pony while on foot.

Individual show A display of your pony's action and paces, carried out in a showing class.

Laminitis Inflammation of the insides of the pony's feet, making them hot and painful.

Leading leg The leg that is in front of the others when the pony is cantering.

Leg up An easy way of getting on a pony, when a helper holds your left leg and pushes you up into the saddle.

Longeing To exercise a horse or pony on a long line that is attached to a special headcollar. It may or may not be ridden at the same time.

Novice A pony or rider that is inexperienced in what it is doing.

Numnah A pad used under the saddle to stop it from rubbing the pony's back.

Paddock Small field in which ponies are kept and sometimes ridden.

Pony nuts A kind of feed made from cereals compressed into small pellets.

Post and rail Fencing made from wooden rails (horizontals) fixed to wooden posts (uprights).

Quarters The back part of a pony—the hindquarters and hind legs.

Reins The parts of the bridle that attach to the bit. You hold the reins in your hands to control the pony.

Rising to the trot Standing up in your stirrups as one pair of the pony's feet hits the ground, and then sitting down as the opposite pair of feet hits .... the ground.

Seat bones The bones that you sit on. You can feel them if you sit on your hands.

Showing Exhibiting a horse or pony at a show, where it is judged on its obedience, paces, and behavior.

Stirrup iron The metal hoop in which you rest your foot when riding.

Straw Hollow stalk of wheat, oats, or barley, used as bedding.

Tack The saddle, bridle, and other equipment used on a pony when it is being ridden.

Trailer A type of wagon in which a horse or pony travels. It is towed by a car.

Travel boots Protective pads that cover the lower legs to prevent injury when traveling.

Trotting rails Poles laid on the ground, spaced so a pony can walk and trot over them.

Index

Notes for Parents and Teachers

Ask children if they think it is extraordinary that an animal as big as a horse or pony can be controlled by a child. Explain that the reason we can do this is because horses and ponies are herd animals that look to the dominant animal in the herd for leadership. When we handle them, we take the place of that dominant animal, and the pony expects to be told what to do.

Horses and ponies are nervous animals, inclined to run away when anything startles them. This is because before they were domesticated, horses lived wild in herds and were preyed upon by predators, such as wolves. Discuss with children how we should handle horses and ponies, bearing this in mind, so as not to frighten them and to gain their trust (i.e. quietly and gently, without a lot of noise).

Taking care of a pony takes up a lot of time and can be very hard work. Ponies need attention at least twice a day, even if they live out in a field. Their diet needs careful regulation, and they like their meals at regular times. Every six to eight weeks their feet need trimming and if they are shod, they will need shoeing. Discuss with children the differences between caring for a pony, and caring for a cat or a dog.

Feeding a pony is very different from feeding most pets. Ponies have a small stomach and large intestines. They need small quantities of food almost constantly passing through their systems, so if they are not out eating grass, they need hay or haylage to chew on. Energy-giving grain feeds must only be provided in small quantities or they will upset the pony's digestion. Explain this to children, and contrast it with the way people eat.

Children may be worried about ponies feeling the more alarming parts of the shoeing process—the burning of the hoof and the hammering in of the nails. Explain that the hoof is just like your fingernails, and that the pony doesn't feel it, any more than you can feel cutting your nails.

Ask children to write a timetable for a day's pony care, starting with feeding in the early morning. They should then include turning the pony out in the field, mucking out the stable, grooming the pony, riding it, bringing it in at night, feeding it, and giving it a final haynet and check. Ask them if they'd like to carry out all these activities every day of the year, including in rain and winter snow.

Belonging to a branch of The Pony Club or to a local riding club teaches children a lot about ponies and riding that they probably would never learn otherwise, especially if their pony is kept at livery, or if they ride a riding-school pony. They can find out the answers to all kinds of questions, from pony care to problem solving, and have tuition in all aspects of riding. It is also an opportunity to make new friends and have fun.

Whatever kind of class the child enters, make sure that they practise with the pony as much as possible, so by the time of the competition, they both know exactly what they are doing. It's best to keep an individual show simple, but to carry out each pace and change of pace as well as possible. Teach the pony to do a good, square halt, with both forefeet and both hind feet in line with each other, and make sure the pony will stand until told to move on again.

Encourage the child to watch other classes, to see how the ponies perform and how well the riders ride them. If a pony is particularly well schooled, see if the child can work out exactly what the rider does to get it to move so well.

When watching jumping classes, point out how many strides different ponies take on approaching a fence. Ask the child to imagine how many strides they would need to take on their pony.

It's fun to construct miniature show jumps at home. Pencils can be painted to make poles, matchboxes to make wall, and small twigs between two pencils tied together with string will make a brush fence. Even if children ride ponies, they will enjoy playing with toy ponies and jumps on a rainy day.

Horse and Pony Websites

www.usef.org
United States Equestrian Federation

www.aqha.com
American Quarter Horse Association

www.horsesport.org
Fédération Equestre Internationale
(The international body that regulates
equestrian sport)

www.horseworlddata.com
General information about horses and
ponies

www.newrider.com
Advice and information for new riders

www.ponyclub.org
The Pony Club

www.worldhorsewelfare.org
World Horse Welfare